Table of Contents

Holiday Dessert Table

Cherry Eggnog Quick Bread

2¹/₂ cups all-purpose flour
³/₄ cup sugar
1 tablespoon baking powder
¹/₂ teaspoon ground nutmeg
1¹/₄ cups prepared dairy eggnog or half-and-half
6 tablespoons butter, melted and cooled
2 eggs, lightly beaten
1 teaspoon vanilla
¹/₂ cup chopped pecans
¹/₂ cup coarsely chopped candied red cherries

1. Preheat oven to 350°F. Grease three 5¹/₂×3-inch mini loaf pans.

2. Combine flour, sugar, baking powder and nutmeg in large bowl. Combine eggnog, melted butter, eggs and vanilla in medium bowl; stir until well blended. Add eggnog mixture to flour mixture. Mix just until all ingredients are moistened. Stir in pecans and cherries. Spoon into prepared pans.

3. Bake 35 to 40 minutes or until wooden toothpick inserted into centers comes out clean. Cool in pans 15 minutes. Remove from pans; cool completely on wire racks. Store tightly wrapped in plastic wrap at room temperature.   *Makes 3 mini loaves*

Note: A loaf of homemade bread makes a great gift—especially when it's given in a new loaf pan. Just add a wooden spoon and the recipe, wrap it all up in a festive towel and tie it with ribbon.

Fireside Steamed Pudding

1½ cups plain dry bread crumbs
1 cup sugar, divided
2 tablespoons all-purpose flour
½ teaspoon baking powder
⅛ teaspoon salt
6 eggs, separated
1 can (21 ounces) cherry pie filling, divided
2 tablespoons butter or margarine, melted
½ teaspoon almond extract
¼ teaspoon red food color
1 cup HERSHEY'S MINI CHIPS™ Semi-Sweet Chocolate Chips
Cherry Whipped Cream (recipe follows)

1. Thoroughly grease 8-cup tube mold or heat-proof bowl.

2. Stir together bread crumbs, ¾ cup sugar, flour, baking powder and salt in large bowl. Stir together egg yolks, 1½ cups cherry pie filling, butter, almond extract and food color in medium bowl; add to crumb mixture, stirring gently until well blended.

3. Beat egg whites in another large bowl until foamy; gradually add remaining ¼ cup sugar, beating until stiff peaks form. Fold about ⅓ beaten egg whites into cherry mixture, blending thoroughly. Fold in remaining egg whites; gently fold in small chocolate chips. Pour batter into prepared tube mold. (If mold is open at top, cover opening with foil and grease top of foil.) Cover mold with wax paper and foil; tie securely with string.

4. Place a rack in large kettle; pour water into kettle to top of rack. Heat water to boiling; place mold on rack. Cover kettle; steam over simmering water about 1½ hours or until wooden pick inserted comes out clean. (Additional water may be needed during steaming.) Remove from heat; cool in pan 5 minutes. Remove cover; unmold onto serving plate. Serve warm with Cherry Whipped Cream.   *Makes 12 to 14 servings*

Cherry Whipped Cream: Beat 1 cup (½ pint) cold whipping cream with ¼ cup powdered sugar in medium bowl until stiff; fold in pie filling remaining from pudding (about ½ cup) and ½ teaspoon almond extract.

Cran-Raspberry Hazelnut Trifle

2 cups hazelnut-flavored liquid dairy creamer
1 package (3.4 ounces) instant vanilla pudding and pie
   filling mix
1 package (about 11 ounces) frozen pound cake, thawed
1 can (21 ounces) raspberry pie filling
1 can (16 ounces) whole berry cranberry sauce

1. Combine dairy creamer and pudding in medium bowl; beat with wire whisk 1 to 2 minutes or until thickened.

2. Cut pound cake into ³⁄₄-inch cubes. Combine pie filling and cranberry sauce in medium bowl; blend well.

3. Layer ¹⁄₃ of cake cubes, ¹⁄₄ of fruit sauce and ¹⁄₃ of pudding mixture in 1¹⁄₂- to 2-quart straight-sided glass serving bowl. Repeat layers twice. Cover; refrigerate until serving time.

Makes 8 servings

Serve It With Style: Garnish trifle with whipped topping, fresh raspberries and fresh mint sprigs.

Prep Time: 20 minutes

Chocolate Raspberry Avalanche Cake

  2 cups all-purpose flour
  2 cups granulated sugar
  6 tablespoons unsweetened cocoa powder
1½ teaspoons baking soda
  1 teaspoon salt
  1 cup hot coffee
  ¾ Butter Flavor CRISCO® Stick or ¾ cup Butter Flavor
     CRISCO® all-vegetable shortening plus additional for
     greasing
  ½ cup milk
  3 eggs
  ¼ cup raspberry-flavored liqueur
     Confectioners' sugar
  1 cup fresh raspberries

1. Heat oven to 350°F. Grease 10-inch (12-cup) Bundt pan with shortening. Flour lightly. Place wire rack on counter for cooling cake.

2. Combine flour, granulated sugar, cocoa, baking soda and salt in large bowl. Add coffee and ¾ cup shortening. Beat at low speed of electric mixer until dry ingredients are moistened. Add milk. Beat at medium speed 1½ minutes. Add eggs, 1 at a time, beating well after each addition. Pour into prepared pan.

3. Bake at 350°F for 40 to 45 minutes, or until toothpick inserted in center comes out clean. *Do not overbake.* Cool 10 minutes before removing from pan. Place cake, fluted side up, on wire rack. Cool 10 minutes. Brush top and side with liqueur. Cool completely. Dust top with confectioners' sugar.

4. Place cake on serving plate. Fill center with raspberries.

Makes 1 (10-inch) cake (12 to 16 servings)

Plum Pudding Pie

- **⅓ cup plus 2 tablespoons KAHLÚA® Liqueur**
- **½ cup golden raisins**
- **½ cup chopped pitted dates**
- **⅓ cup chopped candied cherries**
- **½ cup chopped walnuts**
- **⅓ cup dark corn syrup**
- **½ teaspoon pumpkin pie spice**
- **¼ cup (½ stick) butter or margarine, softened**
- **¼ cup packed brown sugar**
- **2 tablespoons all-purpose flour**
- **¼ teaspoon salt**
- **2 eggs, lightly beaten**
- **1 (9-inch) unbaked pie shell**
- **1 cup whipping cream**
  Maraschino cherries (optional)

In medium bowl, combine ⅓ cup Kahlúa®, raisins, dates and cherries; mix well. Cover; let stand 1 to 4 hours. Stir in walnuts, corn syrup and spice. In large bowl, cream butter, sugar, flour and salt. Stir in eggs. Add fruit mixture; blend well. Pour into unbaked pie shell. Bake in preheated 350°F oven 35 minutes or until filling is firm and crust is golden. Cool completely on wire rack. When ready to serve, in small bowl, beat whipping cream with remaining 2 tablespoons Kahlua® just until soft peaks form. Spoon cream into pastry bag fitted with large star tip and pipe decoratively on top. If desired, garnish with maraschino cherries.   *Makes 8 servings*

Orange Carrot Cake

1 cup (2 sticks) margarine or butter, softened
1 cup GRANDMA'S® Molasses Unsulphured
4 eggs
$\frac{1}{2}$ cup orange juice
1 cup all-purpose flour
1 cup whole wheat flour
2 teaspoons baking soda
1 teaspoon cinnamon
$\frac{1}{2}$ teaspoon salt
2 cups shredded carrots
$\frac{1}{2}$ cup chopped walnuts

FROSTING
1 package (3 ounces) cream cheese, softened
2 tablespoons margarine or butter, softened
1$\frac{1}{2}$ cups powdered sugar
1 teaspoon grated orange peel

Heat oven to 350°F. Grease two 8- or 9-inch round cake pans. In large bowl, combine 1 cup margarine, molasses, eggs and orange juice; mix well. Stir in flours, baking soda, cinnamon and salt; mix well. Stir in carrots and walnuts. Pour into prepared pans. Bake at 350°F 30 to 35 minutes or until toothpick inserted in centers comes out clean. Cool 15 minutes; remove from pans. Cool completely.

In small bowl, combine all frosting ingredients; beat until smooth. Place one cake layer on serving plate; spread top with frosting. Top with second layer; spread top with frosting. If desired, garnish with additional orange peel and walnuts.   *Makes 12 servings*

Chocolate Cheer

Holiday Fudge Torte

  1 cup all-purpose flour
  3/4 cup sugar
  1/4 cup HERSHEY'S Cocoa
  1 1/2 teaspoons powdered instant coffee
  3/4 teaspoon baking soda
  1/4 teaspoon salt
  1/2 cup (1 stick) butter or margarine, softened
  3/4 cup dairy sour cream
  1 egg
  1/2 teaspoon vanilla extract
  Fudge Nut Glaze (recipe follows)

1. Heat oven to 350°F. Grease 9-inch round baking pan; line bottom with wax paper. Grease paper; flour paper and sides of pan.

2. Stir together flour, sugar, cocoa, instant coffee, baking soda and salt in large bowl. Add butter, sour cream, egg and vanilla; beat on low speed of mixer until blended. Increase speed to medium; beat 3 minutes. Pour batter into prepared pan.

3. Bake 30 to 35 minutes or until wooden pick inserted in center comes out clean. Cool 10 minutes. Remove from pan to wire rack; gently peel off wax paper. Cool completely.

4. Prepare Fudge Nut Glaze. Place cake on serving plate; pour glaze evenly over cake, allowing some to run down sides. Refrigerate until glaze is firm, about 1 hour. Cover and refrigerate any leftover torte.   *Makes 8 to 10 servings*

Fudge Nut Glaze: Combine 1/2 cup whipping cream, 1/4 cup sugar, 1 tablespoon butter, 1 1/2 teaspoons light corn syrup and 1/3 cup Hershey's Semi-Sweet Chocolate Chips in small saucepan. Cook over medium heat, stirring constantly, until mixture boils. Cook, stirring constantly, 5 minutes. Remove from heat. Cool 10 minutes; stir in 3/4 cup hazelnuts and 1/2 teaspoon vanilla extract.

Brownie with Ice Cream and Warm Mocha Pecan Sauce

1 package (15½ ounces) brownie mix, plus ingredients to
    prepare mix
½ cup dark brown sugar
½ cup warm water
2 teaspoons instant coffee granules
½ cup unsweetened cocoa powder
¼ teaspoon ground cinnamon
¼ teaspoon ground nutmeg
3 tablespoons butter
1 teaspoon vanilla
⅓ cup pecan pieces
1 pint vanilla or coffee ice cream

1. Prepare and bake brownie mix according to package directions for 9×9-inch baking pan.

2. Combine brown sugar, water and coffee granules in small saucepan. Cook and stir over medium heat until sugar is dissolved. Add cocoa powder, cinnamon and nutmeg. Bring to a simmer, stirring until smooth. Add butter and vanilla; stir until butter is melted. Stir in pecans.

3. Cut brownies into 3×3-inch squares. Place each brownie on serving plate; top with ⅓ cup ice cream. Drizzle 2 tablespoons mocha pecan sauce over each serving.   *Makes 9 servings*

Serving Suggestion: Garnish brownie sundaes with additional pecans.

Chocolate Cake Squares with Eggnog Sauce

1 1/2 **teaspoons baking soda**
   1 **cup buttermilk or sour milk***
   3/4 **cup HERSHEY'S Cocoa**
   3/4 **cup boiling water**
   1/4 **cup (1/2 stick) butter or margarine, softened**
   1/4 **cup shortening**
   2 **cups sugar**
   2 **eggs**
   1 **teaspoon vanilla extract**
   1/8 **teaspoon salt**
1 3/4 **cups all-purpose flour**
   Eggnog Sauce (page 18)

To sour milk: Use 1 tablespoon white vinegar plus milk to equal 1 cup.

1. Heat oven to 350°F. Grease and flour 13×9×2-inch baking pan.

2. Stir baking soda into buttermilk in medium bowl; set aside. Stir together cocoa and water until smooth; set aside.

3. Beat butter, shortening and sugar in large bowl until creamy. Add eggs, vanilla and salt; beat well. Add buttermilk mixture alternately with flour to butter mixture, beating until blended. Add cocoa mixture; blend thoroughly. Pour batter into prepared pan.

4. Bake 40 to 45 minutes or until wooden pick inserted in center comes out clean. Cool completely. Serve with Eggnog Sauce.

Makes 12 to 15 servings

continued on page 18

Chocolate Cake Squares with Eggnog Sauce, continued
Eggnog Sauce

> 1 tablespoon cornstarch
> 2 tablespoons cold water
> 1⅓ cups milk
> ¼ cup sugar
> 3 egg yolks, beaten
> ¼ teaspoon *each* brandy and vanilla extracts
> Several dashes ground nutmeg

Stir cornstarch and water in saucepan until smooth. Add milk, sugar and egg yolks. Beat with whisk until well blended. Cook over medium heat, stirring constantly, until thickened. Remove from heat. Stir in extracts. Cool completely. Sprinkle nutmeg over top. Cover; refrigerate leftover sauce.   *Makes about 1¾ cups sauce*

Easy Fudge Pots de Crème

> 1 package (4-serving size) chocolate cook & serve pudding
>   and pie filling mix*
> 2 cups half-and-half or whole milk
> 1 cup HERSHEY'S Semi-Sweet Chocolate Chips
>   Sweetened whipped cream
>   HERSHEY'S Cocoa (optional)

*Do not use instant pudding mix.

1. Stir together pudding mix and half-and-half in medium saucepan. Cook over medium heat, stirring constantly, until mixture comes to a full boil. Remove from heat.

2. Add chocolate chips; stir until chips are melted and mixture is smooth.

3. Spoon into demitasse cups or small dessert dishes. Press plastic wrap directly onto surface. Refrigerate several hours or until chilled. Garnish with whipped cream; sift cocoa over top, if desired.   *Makes 8 servings*

Almond Fudge Topped Shortbread

1 cup (2 sticks) butter or margarine, softened
½ cup powdered sugar
¼ teaspoon salt
1¼ cups all-purpose flour
2 cups (12-ounce package) HERSHEY¿S Semi-Sweet Chocolate Chips
1 (14-ounce) can sweetened condensed milk (not evaporated milk)
½ teaspoon almond extract
½ cup sliced almonds, toasted

1. Heat oven to 350°F. Grease 13×9×2-inch baking pan.

2. Beat butter, powdered sugar and salt in large bowl until fluffy. Add flour; mix well. With floured hands, press evenly into prepared pan.

3. Bake 20 minutes or until lightly browned.

4. Melt chocolate chips and sweetened condensed milk in heavy saucepan over low heat, stirring constantly. Remove from heat; stir in extract. Spread evenly over baked shortbread. Garnish with almonds; press down firmly. Cool. Chill 3 hours or until firm. Cut into bars. Store covered at room temperature.

Makes 24 to 36 bars

Bavarian Rice Cloud with Bittersweet Chocolate Sauce

1 envelope unflavored gelatin
1 1/2 cups skim milk
3 tablespoons sugar
2 cups cooked rice
2 cups frozen light whipped topping, thawed
1 tablespoon almond-flavored liqueur
1/2 teaspoon vanilla extract
   Vegetable cooking spray
   Bittersweet Chocolate Sauce (recipe follows)
2 tablespoons sliced almonds, toasted

Sprinkle gelatin over milk in small saucepan; let stand 1 minute or until gelatin is softened. Cook over low heat, stirring constantly, until gelatin dissolves. Add sugar and stir until dissolved. Add rice; stir until well blended. Cover and chill until the consistency of unbeaten egg whites. Fold in whipped topping, liqueur, and vanilla. Spoon into 4-cup mold coated with cooking spray. Cover and chill until firm. Unmold onto serving platter. Spoon Bittersweet Chocolate Sauce over rice dessert. Sprinkle with almonds.

Makes 10 servings

Bittersweet Chocolate Sauce

3 tablespoons sugar
3 tablespoons cocoa powder
1/2 cup low-fat buttermilk
1 tablespoon almond-flavored liqueur

Combine sugar and cocoa in small saucepan. Add buttermilk, mixing well. Place over medium heat; cook until sugar dissolves. Stir in liqueur; remove from heat.

Favorite recipe from **USA Rice Federation**

Sweetest Treats

Jingle Bells Chocolate Pretzels

1 cup HERSHEY'S Semi-Sweet Chocolate Chips
1 cup HERSHEY'S Premier White Chips, divided
1 tablespoon plus ½ teaspoon shortening (do not use butter, margarine, spread or oil), divided
About 24 salted or unsalted pretzels (3×2 inches)

1. Cover tray or cookie sheet with wax paper.

2. Place chocolate chips, ⅔ cup white chips and 1 tablespoon shortening in medium microwave-safe bowl. Microwave at HIGH (100%) 1 minute; stir. Microwave at HIGH an additional 1 to 2 minutes, stirring every 30 seconds, until chips are melted when stirred.

3. Using fork, dip each pretzel into chocolate mixture; tap fork on side of bowl to remove excess chocolate. Place coated pretzels on prepared tray.

4. Place remaining ⅓ cup white chips and remaining ½ teaspoon shortening in small microwave-safe bowl. Microwave at HIGH 15 to 30 seconds or until chips are melted when stirred. Using tines of fork, drizzle chip mixture across pretzels. Refrigerate until coating is set. Store in airtight container in cool, dry place.

Makes about 24 coated pretzels

White Dipped Pretzels: Cover tray with wax paper. Place 2 cups (12-ounce package) HERSHEY'S Premier White Chips and 2 tablespoons shortening (do not use butter, margarine, spread or oil) in medium microwave-safe bowl. Microwave at HIGH 1 to 2 minutes or until chips are melted when stirred. Dip pretzels as

continued on page 26

Jingle Bells Chocolate Pretzels, continued

directed on page 24. Place ¼ cup HERSHEY'S Semi-Sweet
Chocolate Chips and ¼ teaspoon shortening (do not use butter,
margarine, spread or oil) in small microwave-safe bowl. Microwave
at HIGH 30 seconds to 1 minute or until chips are melted when
stirred. Drizzle melted chocolate across pretzels, using tines of
fork. Refrigerate and store as directed above.

Chewy Hazelnut Bars

   1 pound DOMINO® Dark Brown Sugar (2⅓ cups, packed)
   ¾ cup (1½ sticks) butter
   2 eggs
   2 teaspoons vanilla
   2 cups all-purpose flour
   2 teaspoons baking powder
   ½ teaspoon salt
   1 cup chopped hazelnuts*
   1 cup semi-sweet chocolate chips
You may substitute pecans or walnuts if desired.

In microwave-safe bowl, heat brown sugar and butter on HIGH
about 2 minutes or until butter melts. Let cool to room temperature.

In medium bowl, beat brown sugar mixture, eggs and vanilla until
well blended. In large bowl, combine flour, baking powder and
salt; add to butter mixture. Stir in nuts and chocolate chips. Spread
mixture evenly into buttered 11×8-inch baking pan. Bake in
preheated 350°F oven 35 to 40 minutes.

Cool completely and cut into 2-inch squares.   *Makes 20 bars*

Pineapple Almond Shortbread Bars

Crust
  1½ cups all-purpose flour
  ½ cup almonds, toasted, ground
  ¼ cup sugar
  ½ cup (1 stick) cold margarine

Topping
  1 can (20 ounces) DOLE® Crushed Pineapple, drained
  3 eggs
  ¼ cup honey
  ¼ cup sugar
  1 tablespoon grated lemon peel
  1½ cups slivered almonds, toasted

For Crust, preheat oven to 350°F. In large bowl, combine flour, almonds and sugar. Cut in margarine until crumbly. Form dough into a ball; press into ungreased 13×9-inch baking pan. Bake 10 minutes. Cool slightly.

For Topping, in medium bowl, combine crushed pineapple, eggs, honey, sugar and lemon peel. Stir in almonds. Pour topping over partially baked crust. Bake an additional 30 to 35 minutes. Cool completely in pan on wire rack. Cut into bars.

Makes about 2 dozen bars

Cranberry Cheese Bars

2 cups all-purpose flour
1½ cups quick-cooking or old-fashioned oats, uncooked
¾ cup plus 1 tablespoon firmly packed light brown sugar, divided
1 cup (2 sticks) butter or margarine, softened
1¾ cups "M&M's"® Chocolate Mini Baking Bits, divided
1 (8-ounce) package cream cheese
1 (14-ounce) can sweetened condensed milk
¼ cup lemon juice
1 teaspoon vanilla extract
2 tablespoons cornstarch
1 (16-ounce) can whole berry cranberry sauce

Preheat oven to 350°F. Lightly grease 13×9×2-inch baking pan; set aside. In large bowl combine flour, oats, ¾ cup sugar and butter; mix until crumbly. Reserve 1½ cups crumb mixture for topping. Stir ½ cup "M&M's"® Chocolate Mini Baking Bits into remaining crumb mixture; press into prepared pan. Bake 15 minutes. Cool completely. In large bowl beat cream cheese until light and fluffy; gradually mix in condensed milk, lemon juice and vanilla until smooth. Pour evenly over crust. In small bowl combine remaining 1 tablespoon sugar, cornstarch and cranberry sauce. Spoon over cream cheese mixture. Stir remaining 1¼ cups "M&M's"® Chocolate Mini Baking Bits into reserved crumb mixture. Sprinkle over cranberry mixture. Bake 40 minutes. Cool at room temperature; refrigerate before cutting. Store in refrigerator in tightly covered container.

Makes 32 bars

Festive Mincemeat Tartlets

Pastry for double pie crust
1½ cups prepared mincemeat
½ cup chopped, peeled and cored tart apple
⅓ cup golden raisins
⅓ cup chopped walnuts
3 tablespoons brandy or frozen apple juice concentrate, thawed
1 tablespoon grated lemon peel

1. Preheat oven to 400°F. Divide pastry in half. Refrigerate one half. Roll remaining half on lightly floured surface to form 13-inch circle. Cut six 4-inch rounds. Fit each pastry round into 2¾-inch muffin cup. Prick inside of crust with fork; set aside. Repeat with remaining pastry.

2. Bake unfilled pastry crusts 8 minutes. Meanwhile, combine mincemeat, apple, raisins, walnuts, brandy and lemon peel in medium bowl until well blended. Remove crusts from oven; fill each with rounded tablespoonful of mincemeat mixture. Press lightly into crust with back of spoon.

3. Bake 18 to 20 minutes more or until crust edges are golden. Cool in pan 5 minutes. Carefully remove from pan to wire rack. Serve warm, or cool completely. *Makes 12 tartlets*

Chocolate-Filled Bonbons

½ **Butter Flavor CRISCO® Stick or ½ cup Butter Flavor**
   CRISCO® all-vegetable shortening
½ **cup granulated sugar**
¼ **cup firmly packed brown sugar**
 1 **egg**
 1 **teaspoon vanilla**
1⅔ **cups all-purpose flour**
½ **teaspoon baking soda**
¼ **teaspoon salt**
36 **small chocolate candies**
36 **nut halves**

1. Heat oven to 400°F. Place sheets of foil on countertop for cooling cookies.

2. Combine shortening, granulated sugar, brown sugar, egg and vanilla in large bowl. Beat at medium speed with electric mixer.

3. Combine flour, baking soda and salt. Stir into creamed mixture.

4. Press two level measuring teaspoonfuls of dough around each chocolate candy, covering candy completely. Place nut half on top of each. Place 2 inches apart on *ungreased* baking sheet.

5. Bake for 6 to 7 minutes. Cookies will not brown. *Do not overbake.* Press nuts gently into hot cookies. Cool on baking sheet 2 minutes on baking sheet. Remove cookies to foil to cool completely.   *Makes 3 dozen cookies*

Caramel-Cinnamon Snack Mix

    2 tablespoons vegetable oil
    ½ cup popcorn kernels
    ½ teaspoon salt, divided
 1 ½ cups packed light brown sugar
    ½ cup (1 stick) butter
    ½ cup corn syrup
    ¼ cup red hot cinnamon candies
    2 cups cinnamon-flavored shaped graham crackers
    1 cup red and green candy-coated chocolate pieces

1. Grease 2 large baking pans; set aside.

2. Heat oil in large saucepan over high heat until hot. Add popcorn kernels. Cover pan. Shake pan constantly over heat until kernels no longer pop. Divide popcorn evenly between 2 large bowls. Add ¼ teaspoon salt to each bowl; toss to coat. Set aside.

3. Preheat oven to 250°F. Combine brown sugar, butter and corn syrup in heavy medium saucepan. Cook over medium heat until sugar melts, stirring constantly with wooden spoon. Bring mixture to a boil. Boil 5 minutes, stirring frequently.

4. Remove ½ of sugar mixture (about ¾ cup) from saucepan; pour over 1 portion of popcorn. Toss with lightly greased spatula until evenly coated.

5. Add red hot candies to saucepan. Stir constantly with wooden spoon until melted. Pour over remaining portion of popcorn; toss with lightly greased spatula until evenly coated.

6. Spread each portion of popcorn in even layer in separate prepared pans with lightly greased spatula.

7. Bake 1 hour, stirring every 15 minutes with wooden spoon to prevent popcorn from sticking together. Cool completely in pans. Combine popcorn, graham crackers and chocolate pieces in large bowl. Store in airtight container at room temperature up to 1 week.   *Makes about 4 quarts*

Tart Cherry and Almond Sugar Plums

1 cup (about 6½ ounces) dried tart cherries
1 cup slivered almonds
5 teaspoons kirsch (cherry liqueur)
⅔ cup coarse white or colored sugar

1. Line medium baking dish with waxed paper; set aside.

2. Place cherries, almonds and kirsch in food processor; process until mixture is finely chopped and comes together.

3. Place sugar in small bowl. Butter hands lightly. Form fruit mixture into 1-inch balls. Roll balls, one at a time, in sugar to coat evenly. Place 1 inch apart in prepared dish. Let stand 20 to 30 minutes or until firm. Cover tightly and refrigerate up to 3 days.

Makes about 20 balls

Cherry Walnut White Chocolate Fudge

   3 cups sugar
   1 cup whipping cream
   ½ cup (1 stick) butter
   ¼ cup light corn syrup
   8 ounces premium white chocolate, chopped
   1 teaspoon vanilla
   1 cup chopped dried cherries
   1 cup toasted walnuts, chopped

1. Spray 9×9-inch pan with nonstick cooking spray; set aside.

2. Spray inside of heavy large saucepan. Combine sugar, whipping cream, butter and syrup in saucepan. Cook over medium heat until sugar dissolves and mixture comes to a boil, stirring frequently. Wash down sugar crystals.

3. Attach candy thermometer to side of pan, making sure bulb is submerged in sugar mixture but not touching bottom of pan. Continue cooking about 6 minutes or until sugar mixture reaches soft-ball stage (234°F) on candy thermometer, stirring frequently. Remove from heat; let stand 10 minutes. (Do not stir.)

4. Add white chocolate and vanilla; stir 1 minute or until chocolate is melted and mixture is smooth. Stir in cherries and walnuts. Spread evenly in prepared pan. Score into 64 squares while fudge is still warm. Refrigerate until firm. Cut along score lines into squares. *Makes 64 candies*

Cookies and Cream Cheesecake Bonbons

24 chocolate cream-filled cookies, divided
1 package (8 ounces) cream cheese, softened
1 cup nonfat dry milk powder
1 teaspoon vanilla
1 pound powdered sugar (about 4 cups)
Fresh raspberries and raspberry leaves for garnish

1. Coarsely chop 12 cookies; set aside.

2. Place remaining 12 cookies in food processor; process until fine crumbs form. Place crumbs on baking sheet lined with waxed paper; set aside.

3. Beat cream cheese, dry milk powder and vanilla in medium bowl with electric mixer at medium speed until smooth. Beat in powdered sugar, 1 cup at a time, at low speed until mixture is smooth. Stir in reserved chopped cookies. Refrigerate 2 hours or until firm.

4. Shape rounded tablespoonfuls cream cheese mixture into balls. Roll balls in reserved cookie crumbs. Garnish, if desired. Store in airtight container in refrigerator.

Makes about 3 dozen bonbons

Taste of Tradition

Colorful Kwanzaa Brownies

¾ cup (1½ sticks) butter or margarine, melted
1½ cups sugar
1½ teaspoons vanilla extract
3 eggs
¾ cup all-purpose flour
½ cup HERSHEY'S Cocoa
½ teaspoon baking powder
¼ teaspoon salt
⅔ cup chopped pecans (optional)
Chocolate Cream (page 42)
Assorted fresh fruit, sliced or cut up

1. Heat oven to 350°F. Grease 12-inch round pizza pan or 13×9×2-inch baking pan.

2. Combine butter, sugar and vanilla in large bowl. Add eggs; beat well with spoon. Combine flour, cocoa, baking powder and salt; gradually stir into egg mixture until blended. Stir in pecans, if desired. Spread batter into prepared pan.

3. Bake 20 to 22 minutes or until top springs back when touched lightly in center. Cool completely. Spread Chocolate Cream over top. Refrigerate about 30 minutes. Garnish with fruit just before serving. Store covered in refrigerator without fruit topping.

Makes 12 to 15 servings

continued on page 42

Colorful Kwanzaa Brownies

Colorful Kwanzaa Brownies, continued
Chocolate Cream

   1 package (8 ounces) cream cheese, softened
   ½ cup sugar
   3 tablespoons HERSHEY'S Cocoa
   1 tablespoon milk
   1½ teaspoons vanilla extract

Beat all ingredients in bowl until smooth.   *Makes about 1 cup*

Hanukkah Fried Cruller Bows

   1¼ cups all-purpose flour
   3 tablespoons powdered sugar
   2 tablespoons granulated sugar
   ½ teaspoon salt
   1 egg
   2 egg whites
   1 teaspoon vanilla
   Vegetable oil for frying
   Powdered sugar and ground cinnamon

1. Combine flour, 3 tablespoons powdered sugar, granulated sugar and salt in small bowl. Stir in egg, egg whites and vanilla with fork until mixture is crumbly.

2. Form dough into ball; knead on lightly floured surface until smooth, about 5 minutes. Cover loosely; let stand about 30 minutes.

3. Heat 2 inches oil to 375°F in large heavy saucepan. Roll dough on floured surface to 12-inch square, about ⅛ inch thick. Cut into 12 (1-inch) strips; cut strips in half to form 24 (6×1-inch) strips. Tie each strip into a knot.

4. Fry knots in oil, a few at a time, 3 to 4 minutes or until golden. Drain on paper towels. Sprinkle with powdered sugar and cinnamon. Serve warm.   *Makes 2 dozen bows*

Western Golden Fruitcake

 1 cup (2 sticks) butter or margarine, softened
 2 cups sugar
 4 eggs
 4 cups all-purpose flour
1½ teaspoons baking soda
 1 cup buttermilk
 ½ cup freshly squeezed SUNKIST® orange juice
 2 cups pecan or walnut halves
 1 package (8 ounces) pitted dates, chopped
 8 ounces candied cherries, halved
 8 ounces candied pineapple chunks
   Grated peel of 2 SUNKIST® fresh oranges
   Fresh Orange or Lemon Glaze (recipes follow)

Preheat oven to 300°F.

In large bowl, cream together butter and sugar. Beat in eggs, 1 at a time. Sift together flour and baking soda. Add to creamed mixture alternately with buttermilk and orange juice, beating until smooth. Stir in nuts, dates, cherries, pineapple and orange peel. Divide batter; spoon 7½ cups into well-greased 10-inch Bundt or tube pan and spoon remaining 2½ cups batter into well-greased small 7½×3½×2¼-inch loaf pan. Bake both cakes 2 hours or until toothpick inserted in center comes out clean. Cool 10 minutes. Remove from pans; cool on wire racks. To serve, drizzle cakes with Fresh Orange or Lemon Glaze and garnish with nut halves, if desired.

Fresh Orange Glaze: In small bowl, combine 1 cup confectioners' sugar, 1 teaspoon freshly grated orange peel and 1½ to 2 tablespoons freshly squeezed orange juice.

Fresh Lemon Glaze: In small bowl, combine 1 cup confectioners' sugar, 1 teaspoon freshly grated lemon peel and 1½ to 2 tablespoons freshly squeezed lemon juice.

Hanukkah Honey Cake

    3 eggs
    ¾ cup packed brown sugar
    ¾ cup vegetable oil
    1¼ cups honey
    ⅔ cup strong coffee
    3 cups all-purpose flour
    1½ teaspoons baking powder
    1 teaspoon baking soda
    ½ teaspoon ground allspice
    ½ teaspoon ground cinnamon
    ½ teaspoon ground nutmeg
    ¾ cup chopped walnuts
    1½ teaspoons grated orange peel
    1 teaspoon grated lemon peel
    2 containers (16 ounces each) vanilla frosting
    Yellow food coloring

Supplies
    1 (13×9-inch) cake board, covered, or large tray
    Pastry bag and medium writing and star tips
    8 small white candles

1. Preheat oven to 325°F. Grease and flour 13×9-inch baking pan.

2. Beat eggs in large bowl at high speed of electric mixer until thick and lemon colored, about 5 minutes. Beat in brown sugar and oil. Add honey and coffee; stir well. Combine flour, baking powder, baking soda and spices in small bowl; add to batter and stir well. Stir in walnuts and grated peels. Pour into prepared pan.

3. Bake 40 to 45 minutes until cake is golden and wooden toothpick inserted into center comes out clean. Cool in pan on wire rack 15 minutes. Remove from pan to rack; cool.

4. If cake top is rounded, trim horizontally with long serrated knife. Place cake on prepared cake board. Frost top and sides of cake with 1 container frosting.

continued on page 46

Hanukkah Honey Cake, continued

5. Using photo as guide (page 45), cut pattern from waxed paper. Position pattern on cake as shown in photo. Trace around pattern with wooden toothpick; remove pattern.

6. Tint remaining container frosting yellow. To tint frosting, add small amount of desired food coloring; stir well. Slowly add more coloring until frosting is desired shade. Spoon frosting into pastry bag fitted with medium writing tip. Outline menorah pattern with frosting. Using star tip, fill in menorah and pipe decorative border around edge of cake. Insert candles.   *Makes 12 to 14 servings*

Orange Glazed Pound Cake

**1 package DUNCAN HINES® Moist Deluxe® Butter Recipe
    Golden Cake Mix**
4 eggs
1 cup sour cream
⅓ cup vegetable oil
¼ cup plus 1 to 2 tablespoons orange juice, divided
2 tablespoons grated orange peel
1 cup confectioners' sugar

1. Preheat oven to 375°F. Grease and flour 10-inch tube pan.

2. Combine cake mix, eggs, sour cream, oil, ¼ cup orange juice and orange peel in large bowl. Beat at medium speed with electric mixer for 2 minutes. Pour into prepared pan. Bake at 375°F for 45 to 50 minutes or until toothpick inserted in center comes out clean. Cool in pan 25 minutes. Invert onto cooling rack. Cool completely.

3. Combine sugar and remaining 1 to 2 tablespoons orange juice in small bowl; stir until smooth. Drizzle over cake. Garnish as desired.   *Makes 12 to 16 servings*

New Year's Light

Winter Fruit Compote

1 can (16 ounces) pitted dark sweet cherries in syrup,
    undrained
1 teaspoon cornstarch
1 tablespoon almond-flavored liqueur *or* ½ teaspoon almond
    extract
1½ tablespoons honey
2 ripe Bartlett or Comice pears, peeled, cored and cut into
    1-inch cubes
1 teaspoon chopped fresh mint
Mint sprigs (optional)

1. Drain cherries reserving ¼ cup liquid. Combine reserved liquid
and cornstarch in small bowl; mix until smooth. Add mixture to
saucepan and bring to a boil, over medium-high heat; stirring
frequently. Reduce heat to simmer and as mixture begins to thicken,
stir in liqueur and honey.

2. Stir in pears and drained cherries. Cook 2 minutes or until fruit
is warm, stirring occasionally. Spoon into dessert dishes; sprinkle
with mint and garnish with mint sprigs, if desired. Serve warm or
at room temperature. *Makes 4 servings*

Lemon Pudding Soufflés

1 cup sugar, divided
¼ cup all-purpose flour
⅛ teaspoon salt
¼ cup Dried Plum Purée (recipe follows)
1 egg yolk
⅓ cup fresh lemon juice
  Grated peel of 1 lemon
1 cup nonfat milk
4 egg whites
  Powdered sugar
  Lemon peel, for garnish

Preheat oven to 350°F. Coat eight 5-ounce custard cups with vegetable cooking spray. In mixer bowl, combine ¾ cup sugar, flour and salt until blended. Beat in dried plum purée until well blended. Add egg yolk, lemon juice and lemon peel; mix well. Add milk; mix until well blended. In another mixer bowl, with clean beaters, beat egg whites until soft peaks form. Gradually beat in the remaining ¼ cup sugar until stiff peaks form. Mix one fourth of egg white mixture into lemon mixture; fold in the remaining egg white mixture. Spoon batter into prepared custard cups, dividing equally. Set cups in shallow pan and add ½ inch boiling water to pan. Bake in center of oven 45 to 50 minutes until puffy, set and browned. Cool 10 minutes. Dust with powdered sugar and garnish with lemon peel. Serve hot.   *Makes 8 servings*

Dried Plum Purée: Combine 1⅓ cups (8 ounces) pitted dried plums and 6 tablespoons hot water in container of food processor or blender. Pulse on and off until dried plums are finely chopped and smooth. Store leftovers in a covered container in the refrigerator for up to two months. Makes 1 cup.

Favorite recipe from **California Dried Plum Board**

Confetti New Year's Resolution Cookies

Ingredients
- ⅓ **cup all-purpose flour**
- 6 **tablespoons sugar**
- 1 **tablespoon cornstarch**
- ⅛ **teaspoon salt**
- ⅓ **cup water**
- ¼ **cup vegetable oil**
- 1 **egg white**
- 1 **teaspoon vanilla**
- **Assorted food colorings**

Supplies
Prepared resolutions*

Type resolutions (or write them in pencil, not ink) on 2×½-inch pieces of paper. Be sure to have all your resolutions prepared ahead of time because you must work quickly once you start making the cookies. Here are some ideas to get you started: I will smile more; Reduce, reuse, recycle; I resolve to be kinder to fellow humans; Live long and prosper; I will make my first million before I'm 30 (40?, 50?).

1. Combine flour, sugar, cornstarch and salt in small bowl. Add water, oil, egg white and vanilla; stir until smooth. Divide into 3 bowls. Use 1 or 2 drops food coloring to tint batter in each bowl.

2. Grease small skillet. Heat over medium heat. Spoon 1 tablespoon batter into pan, spreading to 3-inch circle with back of spoon. Cook 5 minutes or until golden brown on bottom. Turn over; cook 1 minute.

3. Remove cookie from skillet and place, darker side up, on flat surface. Immediately place prepared resolution in center of cookie. Fold cookie in half. Fold over edge of bowl.

4. Place in muffin pan to hold shape while cooling. Repeat with remaining batter.   *Makes 3 dozen cookies*

Individual Orange Soufflés

3 oranges
1½ tablespoons cornstarch
3 tablespoons orange-flavored liqueur
6 egg whites
⅛ teaspoon salt
6 tablespoons granulated sugar
1½ tablespoons sliced almonds (optional)
1½ tablespoons powdered sugar (optional)

1. Preheat oven to 450°F. Spray 6 individual soufflé dishes (8 to 10 ounces each) with nonstick cooking spray. Place dishes on jelly-roll pan.

2. Grate enough orange peel to equal 1½ teaspoons; set aside. Remove peel and membrane from oranges; section oranges. Dice oranges; place in small saucepan. (Saucepan should contain 1½ cups juice and pulp.)

3. Stir in cornstarch until smooth. Cook and stir over medium heat until mixture comes to a boil and thickens slightly. Remove from heat; stir in liqueur and reserved orange peel.

4. Beat egg whites and salt with electric mixer at high speed in large bowl until soft peaks form.

5. Gradually beat in granulated sugar, 1 tablespoon at a time, until stiff peaks form and sugar is dissolved.

6. Fold ¼ of egg white mixture into orange mixture. Fold orange mixture into remaining egg white mixture. Spoon into prepared dishes; sprinkle with almonds, if desired.

7. Immediately bake 12 to 15 minutes or until soufflés are puffed and browned. Sprinkle with powdered sugar, if desired. Serve immediately. *Makes 6 servings*

Rustic Cranberry-Pear Galette

¼ cup granulated sugar, divided
1 tablespoon plus 1 teaspoon cornstarch
2 teaspoons ground cinnamon or apple pie spice
4 cups peeled, thinly sliced Bartlett pears
¼ cup dried cranberries
1 teaspoon vanilla
¼ teaspoon almond extract (optional)
1 refrigerated pie crust, at room temperature
1 egg white
1 tablespoon water

1. Preheat oven to 450°F. Coat pizza pan or baking sheet with nonstick cooking spray; set aside.

2. Combine all but 1 teaspoon sugar, cornstarch and cinnamon in medium bowl; blend well. Add pears, cranberries, vanilla and almond extract; toss to coat.

3. Remove crust from pouch; unfold crust and remove plastic sheets. Place on prepared pan. Spoon pear mixture in center of crust to within 2 inches from edge. Fold edge of crust 2 inches over pear mixture; crimp slightly.

4. Combine egg white and water in small bowl; whisk until well blended. Brush outer edges of pie crust with egg white mixture; sprinkle with remaining 1 teaspoon sugar.

5. Bake 25 minutes or until pears are tender and crust is golden brown. If edges brown too quickly, cover with foil after 15 minutes of baking. Cool on wire rack 30 minutes.   *Makes 8 servings*

Candied Citrus Peel

6 large, thick-skinned oranges
13½ cups water
5 cups sugar, divided

1. Remove peel from white part of oranges in long strips with sharp paring knife. Reserve fruit for another use. Discard all pithy fruit membranes from peel. Cut peel into 2×½-inch strips. (There will be some oddly shaped pieces.) Place sheet of waxed paper under wire rack. Bring 4 cups water to a boil in heavy 3-quart saucepan over high heat. Add peel; return to a boil. Reduce heat to low. Cover; cook 20 minutes. Drain. Repeat process 2 times.

2. Bring 4½ cups sugar and 1½ cups water to a boil in same saucepan over medium heat, stirring occasionally. Reduce heat to low. Carefully clip candy thermometer to side of pan (do not let bulb touch bottom of pan). Cook over low heat about 20 minutes or until thermometer registers 230°F, without stirring. Add drained peel. Cook over low heat about 20 minutes more or until thermometer registers 240°F (soft-ball stage), stirring occasionally. Remove from heat. Remove strips with slotted spoon to wire rack over waxed paper. Discard syrup or save for another use. Cool strips until syrup has dripped off.

3. Put remaining ½ cup sugar on another sheet of waxed paper. Roll strips, one at a time, in sugar. Set strips on wire rack about 1 hour or until dry. Store in airtight container. Keep in a cool place up to 2 weeks. If strips become slightly sticky, roll again in additional sugar. *Makes about 90 strips*

Variation: Melt ½ cup semisweet chocolate chips and 1 tablespoon butter in small saucepan over low heat, stirring until smooth. Dip one end of each strip in melted chocolate; set on wire rack over waxed paper to dry. Let chocolate set completely before storing in airtight container.

A Lighter Chocolate Decadence

1¼ cups sugar, divided
⅔ cup unsweetened cocoa powder
2 tablespoons all-purpose flour
¾ cup nonfat milk
5 ounces (about ¾ cup) semisweet chocolate chips
¼ cup Dried Plum Purée (page 50)
1 egg
1 egg yolk
1 teaspoon vanilla
2 egg whites
⅛ teaspoon cream of tartar
Raspberry Sauce (page 60)
1½ cups low-fat nondairy whipped topping
Fresh raspberries and mint leaves for garnish

Preheat oven to 350°F. Line 9-inch cake pan with waxed paper; coat with cooking spray. In medium saucepan, combine 1 cup sugar, cocoa and flour. Slowly whisk in milk until blended. Bring to a simmer over low heat, stirring constantly. Place chocolate chips in large bowl; pour in hot mixture, stirring until chocolate melts. Whisk in Dried Plum Purée, egg, egg yolk and vanilla until blended. Set aside to cool. In mixer bowl, beat egg whites with cream of tartar until foamy. Gradually beat in remaining ¼ cup sugar until stiff peaks form. Fold half the egg white mixture into cooled chocolate mixture; fold in remaining egg white mixture. Pour into prepared pan. Bake in center of oven 30 to 35 minutes until puffy and center is set but still moist. (Do not overbake.) Cool completely in pan on wire rack. (Cake will sink as it cools.) Remove from pan. Wrap securely; chill 24 hours before serving. Prepare Raspberry Sauce. Cut dessert into wedges; serve with sauce and whipped topping. Garnish with raspberries and mint leaves.

Makes 12 servings

continued on page 60

A Lighter Chocolate Decadence, continued

Raspberry Sauce: Purée 1 package (12 ounces) thawed frozen raspberries in blender; strain to remove seeds. Sweeten to taste with sugar. Makes 1 cup.

Favorite recipe from **California Dried Plum Board**

Raspberry Cheese Tarts

Crust
   1¼ cups graham cracker crumbs
   5 tablespoons light margarine (50% less fat and calories)
   ¼ cup SPLENDA® No Calorie Sweetener, Granular

Filling
   4 ounces reduced-fat cream cheese
   ½ cup plain nonfat yogurt
   1 cup SPLENDA® No Calorie Sweetener, Granular
   ½ cup egg substitute
   1 cup frozen raspberries

Crust

1. Preheat oven to 350°F. In medium bowl, mix together graham cracker crumbs, margarine and ¼ cup SPLENDA®. Press about 1 tablespoon of crust mixture into 10 muffin pan cups lined with paper liners. Set aside.

Filling

2. In small bowl, beat cream cheese with electric mixer on low speed until soft, about 30 seconds. Add yogurt; beat on low speed until smooth. Stir in SPLENDA® and egg substitute until well blended.

3. Place 1½ tablespoons raspberries into each muffin cup. Divide filling evenly among muffin cups. Bake for 20 minutes or until firm. Refrigerate for 2 hours before serving.   *Makes 10 servings*

The publisher would like to thank the companies and organizations listed below for the use of their recipes and photographs in this publication.

California Dried Plum Board

Crisco is a registered trademark of The J.M. Smucker Company

Dole Food Company, Inc.

Domino® Foods, Inc.

Duncan Hines® and Moist Deluxe® are registered trademarks of Pinnacle Foods Corp.

Grandma's® is a registered trademark of Mott's, LLP

Hershey Foods Corporation

Kahlúa® Liqueur

© Mars, Incorporated 2005

SPLENDA® is a trademark of McNeil Nutritionals, LLC

Reprinted with permission of Sunkist Growers, Inc.

USA Rice Federation